MEDICAL PRACTICES
in the CIVIL WAR

Other books by Susan Provost Beller:

Roots for Kids: A Genealogy Guide for Young People
Cadets at War: The True Story of Teenage Heroism at the
    Battle of New Market
Woman of Independence: The Life of Abigail Adams
Mosby and His Rangers: Adventures of the Gray Ghost

MEDICAL PRACTICES in the CIVIL WAR

SUSAN PROVOST BELLER

BETTERWAY BOOKS
Cincinnati, Ohio

Cover design by Brian Roeth
Typography by Blackhawk Typesetting

Medical Practices in the Civil War. Copyright © 1992 by Susan Provost Beller. Printed and bound in the United States of America. All rights reserved. No part of this book may be reproduced in any form or by any electronic or mechanical means including information storage and retrieval systems without permission in writing from the publisher, except by a reviewer, who may quote brief passages in a review. Published by Betterway Books, an imprint of F&W Publications, Inc., 1507 Dana Avenue, Cincinnati, Ohio 45207. 1-800-289-0963. First edition.

99 98 97 96 95 6 5 4 3 2

Library of Congress Cataloging-in-Publication Data

Beller, Susan Provost.
Medical practices in the Civil War / Susan Provost Beller.
    p. cm.
    Includes bibliographical references and index.
    Summary: Discusses medical care during the Civil War, focusing on disease, wounds, medical personnel, instruments, surgery and anesthesia, recovery, and changes in medicine during the war.
    ISBN 1-55870-264-4
    1. United States—History—Civil War, 1861-1865—Medical care-Juvenile literature. [1. United States—History—Civil War, 1861-1865—Medical care.] I. Title.
E621.B55 1992
973.7'75—dc20   92-14960
                                         CIP
                                         AC

This book is dedicated to my daughter, Jennifer Erin Beller, who loves all things medical.

ACKNOWLEDGMENTS

One of my favorite parts of writing a book is when the book is completed and I have the chance to say thank you to the people who helped make it possible. In researching books, I have met new friends and they have shared in the process of making my ideas real. In writing this book, I had the privilege of working with Jan Lazarus in the Prints and Photographs Division at the National Library of Medicine, who was a great help even in the situations where I wasn't sure what I wanted. Mike Rhode is the Archivist of the Otis Historical Archives at the National Museum of Health and Medicine. His knowledge of the photographs in his collection made my job of selecting photos much easier than it could have been. Alan Hawk manages the Historical Collections for the same museum. He not only provided photographs of items in the collection, but also gave me a great tour of the collection and let me hold some of the medical equipment. His enthusiasm for everything in the collection, even for embalming equipment, was catching.

Closer to home, three libraries are deserving of my thanks for their assistance in making this book possible. My thanks go to Bobbi Hirsch of the Waterbury

Village Public Library, who invited me to look at and photograph all of Dr. Henry Janes's medical memorabilia. The Special Collections Department at the University of Vermont's Bailey-Howe Library was the source of Dr. Janes's records of his Civil War cases, along with some old medical textbooks of the era. Kathy Goddard of the University of Vermont's Dana Medical Library helped with providing a copy of the *Medical and Surgical History* and more Civil War era textbooks. Again, my thanks.

My readers this time included my three children, Mike, Jennie, and Sean. I must be getting better since they found fewer things to criticize than usual. ("At least you put verbs in all your sentences this time!") My colleague at the Bristol Elementary School library, Dee Corkins, offered many suggestions and corrections that I know improved the manuscript. My husband, W. Michael Beller, again served as a "detail" reader, painstakingly catching the grammar and wording errors. He also is responsible for making me finally understand the difference between a smooth bore and a rifled musket. His photographs of the items at the Waterbury Village Public Library also add much to the story of Dr. Janes.

CONTENTS

Introduction 11

1. One Doctor's Story 13

2. Living and Dying, the Terrible Numbers . 17

3. Medical Knowledge of the 1860s 19

4. Dying from Disease 23

5. Dying from Wounds 27

6. People of Medicine —
   Surgeons and Stewards 33

7. People of Medicine —
   Nurses and Other Staff 39

8. Transportation from Battlefield
   to Hospital 47

9. Hospitals 51

10. The Wounded Soldier: Field Hospital to
    General Hospital 57

11. Medical Instruments 63

12. Surgery... 67

13. Anesthesia 71

14. Medicines 75

15. Recovery 79

16. Death 83

17. Changes in Medicine during
    the Civil War 85

Sources for Research 89

Index 93

INTRODUCTION

The story of medicine during the Civil War that is told here comes from a different story of the Civil War, which I have told to numerous school groups. While telling students the story of the Virginia Military Institute cadets at the Battle of New Market, I have to tell of the death of one cadet, who was not badly wounded in the battle but died horribly six weeks later from tetanus. As I explain that his tetanus was probably caused by his doctor using dirty instruments, my listeners always seem to come up with the same questions, such as: "Why didn't they wash their instruments?" and "Why didn't the doctors just give him a shot to make him better?" They are fascinated with the medical knowledge, or rather the lack of medical knowledge, of doctors at the time of the Civil War. They cannot imagine a world without antibiotics and clean hospitals and all of the medical technology that we take for granted today. The story of medical care during the Civil War rapidly becomes a focus for my audience's interest, yet I never have time to explain it as fully as I'd like to.

This book tells that interesting and fascinating story, including pictures, since this is a story the students would NEVER believe without "proof." I would like to have these readers read and see for themselves how very different medicine was during the Civil War.

And now, for the unbelievable but TRUE story ...

Chapter 1

ONE DOCTOR'S STORY

The date was November 19, 1863. The place was Gettysburg, Pennsylvania. Five and one-half months before, what would become known as the most important battle in the Civil War had taken place here. Now a cemetery was being dedicated to the memory of the many soldiers who never left that battlefield on those three days in July. A famous orator, Edward Everett, and the President of the United States, Abraham Lincoln, had come to speak at this dedication. This ceremony would give the nation a chance to honor all of the soldiers who had already given their lives in this long war. Sitting on the speaker's platform listening to Abraham Lincoln give his short but famous Gettysburg Address was a Vermonter. His name was Henry Janes, and he was the man responsible for the care of all the soldiers who were left wounded on the battlefield when the three days of fighting had ended.

Born in Waterbury, Vermont on January 24, 1832, Henry Janes received his M.D. degree in 1855 and began a medical practice in his hometown in 1857. When the 3rd Vermont Volunteers were organized in 1861, Henry Janes became their surgeon. He would have a very successful military career and find himself in charge of large Union hospitals after many major campaigns of the Civil War. He did not stay with the 3rd Vermont for long. Very soon he was named a surgeon in the U.S. Army. After the battle of Gettysburg, he was appointed surgeon in charge of all army hospitals in the area, where he was responsible for the care of over 20,000 wounded soldiers, both Union and Confederate.

In the archives at the University of Vermont, you can spend hours reading through his records of the cases he treated after this battle, and also of the wounded soldiers put under his supervision when most of the army left a few days after the battle. His notes came from the bed cards of the patients. The entries are arranged by the battle in which the soldiers were wounded and then by the type of injury. He gives their name, age, company and regiment, the date they were admitted to the hospital's care, the date of injury, the date of any operation, and then a closing date according to whether they were discharged as "cured" or "not cured" or a date of death. His comments on each case are clinical but often add a homey touch. For Vermonter Daniel Jones, age twenty-three, wounded at Cedar Creek, he adds, "General health good and just married."

Dr. Janes's sympathy for the suffering of the wounded comes through in his notes. What is also evident is some of his frustration. In the days immediately after the battle, his hospital was mostly for the cases that could not be cared for and moved right away. These were already difficult cases, and it must have been frustrating to watch them die. His notes on a Georgia soldier, age thirty-five, listed only as F. Darcy, show his helplessness: "The patient at first seemed as like to recover as the two following cases but he soon began to sink and died on the 11th day after injury." He was willing to try any technique to save his patients. Seventeen-year-old Lucius Britton, a Confederate soldier from Mississippi who was wounded at Gettysburg, has this recorded in the notes of his care: "Acupuncture was resorted to with success." And when the jaw of a thirty-eight-year-old Alabama soldier, Thomas McLaughlin, became locked from tetanus, Dr. Janes reported that "A tooth was extracted and through this opening the patient was fed." His sympathy and understanding seem as genuine for the enemy soldiers as for those of the Union (with, of course, the exception of his special attention to his Vermonters!).

Dr. Janes also had to deal with a number of administrative problems as head of the military hospitals after the battle of Gettysburg. The *Official Records*, which contain all the messages and reports of the military

Uniform, boots, belt, and camp trunk used by Dr. Henry Janes, surgeon to the Third Vermont Regiment. These are now on display in the bedroom of his home, now the Waterbury Village Public Library. (Photo by W. Michael Beller.)

15

leaders during the Civil War, includes some of Dr. Janes's requests for equipment in order to meet the needs of his patients. He wrote to the Medical Director of the Army of the Potomac on July 9, 1863: "The number of wounded here probably exceeded 20,000. We have been short of nurses, surgeons, and transportation, both ambulances and railroad. I shall be able to begin the permanent hospital soon, if I can get the hospital tents. There are not enough in the corps hospitals for the purpose." Five days later, he wrote again, "Am anxiously awaiting the tents." The records don't show when the tents finally did arrive. The final medical report on the battle, which is in the *Official Records*, praises the handling of the wounded and the dedication of the medical officers: "When other officers had time to rest, they were busily at work — and not merely at work, but working earnestly and devotedly."

Dr. Henry Janes returned to Vermont to serve as the surgeon in charge of a long-term military hospital in Montpelier. At the end of the Civil War, he returned to his practice in Waterbury, Vermont, where he lived until his death in 1915, at age eighty-two. His home and office in Waterbury is the location today of the Waterbury Village Public Library, as he wished. But upstairs in his old bedroom are preserved all the articles he kept from his military service — his uniform, boots, and camp trunk. His medical instruments and medical kits, including the ammunition case that he converted to carry medicines with him in battle, are kept in glass cases.

Henry Janes was just one surgeon, though an important one, who served his country during the horrible days of the Civil War. His story is just a tiny part of a bigger story about living and dying for the soldiers who fought in this war.

Chapter 2

LIVING AND DYING,
THE TERRIBLE NUMBERS

When you total up the numbers of all the soldiers who died during the Civil War, the sums are terrible. Over two and one-half million soldiers fought for the Union during the Civil War. Of that number, about 360,000 soldiers died. Probably over one million soldiers fought for the Confederacy during the long war; about 258,000 died.

What is most unbelievable, though, is that of those 618,000 deaths, only 200,000 were the result of either being killed or wounded in a battle or skirmish. That means only one out of every three soldiers who died during the Civil War died from being wounded or killed in the fighting. The other two out of three deaths were from disease. These deaths were not from being shot or even from the infections that soldiers sometimes developed while recuperating from being shot. Lockjaw was one disease wounded soldiers sometimes died from because of the dirty medical instruments used at that time.

Two out of every three soldiers who died during the Civil War died from diseases like measles, mumps, diarrhea, pneumonia, and typhoid fever. These soldiers died because doctors then didn't know how important it was that camps where the soldiers lived be kept clean. They didn't know that eating the right foods and keeping clean would help protect soldiers from disease. The soldiers died because doctors didn't know that simple diseases would spread horribly fast in the overcrowded camps. They also died because doctors didn't have the kinds of medicines that we take for granted today. There were no antibiotics to fight infections. There were no vaccines to give to children to protect them for life against things like mumps, measles, and tetanus — diseases that children today receive immunizations for so that they will never have to suffer from the disease.

It is hard for us to believe that there was ever a time when people didn't know all these simple practices for taking care of themselves. But it is necessary to understand that this was so in order to understand why doctors during the Civil War were not able to prevent these soldiers from dying. The first place to start is to look at what doctors knew about disease and about taking care of wounds during the Civil War. Some of the things doctors believed about caring for patients at that time will amaze you!

Chapter 3

MEDICAL KNOWLEDGE
OF THE 1860S

*O*f all instruments for conducting an examination of a gunshot wound, the finger of the surgeon is most appropriate. T. Longmore, the author of an 1863 book entitled *A Treatise on Gunshot Wounds*, goes on to say that a finger is also better for removing the bullet and small pieces of cloth and dirt from the wound. Many other doctors of the time would not have disagreed. This was normal practice at a time when doctors only rarely bothered washing their hands at all. They never stopped to wash the blood of one patient from their hands or to clean off their clothes before going on to the next patient. Even their instruments, which they used when the fingers just couldn't do the job, were only washed at the end of the day. What doctors didn't know in the 1860s killed many patients during the Civil War.

Reading through the old medical books can be a very interesting experience. It is amazing to read about the things doctors thought were effective compared to what we know today. Some of the things they didn't know are shocking. But overall, the reader comes away impressed with their common sense approach to medical care.

It's important to understand that many Civil War surgeons had never even seen an operation done before the Civil War. Most of them listened to two years of

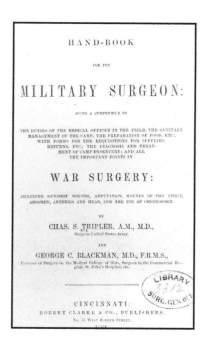

Title page from a Military Surgery textbook widely used by Union Army surgeons. (National Library of Medicine.)

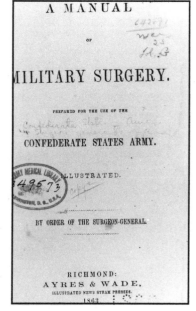

Title page from textbook prepared by the Confederate Surgeon General's Office for use by Confederate surgeons. (National Library of Medicine.)

medical lectures and read whatever books about medicine were available. Then they went out and learned medicine by working with doctors already in practice.

The books they read were a mix of good advice and absolutely terrible advice. Take, for example, Longmore's recommendation to use one's fingers to remove a Minié ball from a wound. Today that advice sounds horrible because we know of all the germs we have on our hands. Even young children today are taught to wash their hands often. However, we need to remember that even surgeons in the 1860s washed their hands occasionally, which was more than they did for their medical instruments. Surgeons wore large aprons to protect their street clothes and just wiped their instruments off on the front of their dirty aprons. They didn't care if the instruments were dirty as long as they were sharp so that they could cut well. So maybe using their fingers was safer for the patients than using their instruments.

Another horrible piece of advice that shows up in all the medical texts of that time is about "laudable pus." All the books said that signs of pus coming from a wound three or four days after injury or surgery was a sign of healing. In actual fact, the pus was a sign of severe bacterial infection caused by the doctors' dirty hands and instruments. Yet every medical book praised "laudable pus" as a sign that the body was healing itself.

If there was one most important piece of information that was missing from doctors' knowledge at the time, it was knowledge about how disease was transmitted. Doctors didn't know about bacteria and viruses. They didn't know that people could become sick from other people's dirty hands or from breathing other people's germs in a crowded tent or a hospital ward.

But reading the medical books of the 1860s also shows what doctors were starting to learn about proper treatment of the sick and wounded. Along with the bad advice comes this from Dr. Edward Warren, a famous Confederate surgeon: "Recovery and comfort are both promoted by a regular temperature, free ventilation, cleanliness of body, words of encouragement and kindness, clean and comfortable bedding."

Doctors were telling the army leaders that their patients and all soldiers needed good, fresh food, that their tents should not be set up on wet, marshy soil, and that soldiers should not have to march more than fifteen miles a day. Doctors were recommending rest breaks at midday for soldiers to wash their feet, and that soldiers carry as little weight as possible on the march. One surgeon stated bluntly that "Cleanliness is the life of an army while filth and dirt are among its disease-generating causes." Unfortunately, the army leadership, desperately busy trying to fight the war, didn't have time to take advantage of even the little good advice that doctors could offer them.

So medical knowledge during Civil War times was a mix of good advice and ignorance. Considering how little doctors knew, what most people find most amazing is how many people survived being ill or wounded during the Civil War. One of the more famous stories of survival in spite of all the odds during the Civil War is the story of Samuel C. Wright, from Massachusetts. This soldier was involved in twenty-one different battles and, over the years, was wounded enough times to kill several soldiers. During the course of his military service in the Union Army, he received two head wounds, was shot in both of his legs and one of his arms, lost an eye from one wound, broke one of his legs in battle, had typhoid fever, and was run over by an army wagon. Sam not only survived the Civil War, but lived to the ripe old age of seventy-nine.

Chapter 4

DYING FROM DISEASE

s soon after enlistment as possible, the recruit is hurried to the depot; he is supplied with army rations badly cooked and uncleanly served; he is drilled vigorously several hours each day; at night, furnished with one or two blankets and occasionally a little straw, he is thrust into a tent with a large number of others, or into crowded temporary quarters, where he is subjected to horribly impure air, frequently to cold and dampness, and always to excessive discomfort, or he is required to perform a tour of guard duty which interrupts his habit of nightly repose; but slender opportunities of washing and bathing are afforded him, and he is at all times exposed to the influences of the unwholesome air of badly-policed camps and quarters, and to the emanations from his comrades suffering under various contagious maladies.

Dr. Roberts Bartholow, a former assistant surgeon in the Union army, wrote these words in 1867. He was writing a report that would be part of a book by the U.S. Sanitary Commission on why so many soldiers died from disease during the Civil War. Remember those numbers from Chapter 2. Over 60% of the deaths from the Civil War came from disease, not from being wounded in battle.

Those numbers seem horrible even to think of. But the doctors writing for the Sanitary Commission report were actually happy about these numbers. One doctor talks proudly of the fact that *only* two out of every three deaths were from disease. He talks about the U.S. Army troops who fought in the Mexican War in 1848. Dr. Dunster says that in that war, seven out of every eight deaths were from disease. He is proud that the percentage had been brought down from 88% to only 62% in the Civil War.

But why did so many men die from disease? Let's look at those things that Dr. Bartholow mentioned. What he said breaks down into three main causes of the diseases that were so common during the Civil War: bad food, overcrowded conditions of the camps, and lack of personal cleanliness.

The bad food of the Civil War has become one of the most talked about topics in all the memoirs written by soldiers in the years after the war ended. Especially as the war went on longer and longer, the food got worse and worse. Some of this was because of how hard it was to get the food to the soldiers. Often there was food but it was not where the soldiers were. This was especially true when the armies were on the march because their supply wagons couldn't keep up with them. Some of it was because there were people who took advantage of the wartime conditions and sold inedible food to the military. In the South, towards the end of the war, there just wasn't enough food left for anyone anymore, including the soldiers.

Soldiers added to their official "diet" from several sources. One was food from home. Another was provisions given out by the Sanitary Commission. Some soldiers became scavengers, taking food wherever they could get it. Northerners, living on Virginia soil, felt it was their right to take any supplies they could from the Southerners, since they were the enemy. Other Union soldiers ate meals at the homes of Southerners, paying for their hospitality. Soldiers also could get food from the sutlers, who were independent merchants following after the armies and selling goods from their wagons. Since most of the fighting was on Southern soil, Southern soldiers had the most luck getting food from the residents. It was just as well that they did. Otherwise, as their army rations became more and more scarce, they never would have had enough to live on.

Another problem with the food was that it was poorly stored and then badly cooked, leading to disease from eating rotten food. Also, soldiers might have very little to eat for several days and then, when the wagons arrived, they would stuff themselves. Going back and forth between starvation and gorging themselves was not good for their health. In addition, the food that they had was often not what that their bodies needed. During the Civil War, there were several severe outbreaks of scurvy. Scurvy comes from a lack of the vitamins we get in fresh fruits and vegetables. Many doctors of the time ordered fruits and vegetables for the soldiers, knowing it would prevent the outbreak of scurvy. But at least one, whose report is in the U.S. Sanitary Commission record, ordered that the men be given "fresh and pure blood" from animals to make them better.

Dr. Bartholow's second reason for the cause of disease among the soldiers was the overcrowding of the soldiers both in camp and in the hospitals. Doctors didn't know then how diseases travel from person to person. With so many people becoming ill, it was inevitable that all the diseases would spread through the crowded camps. The official Surgeon General's report on the Civil War says that about 57,000 people died during the Civil War from diarrhea or dysentery. Diseases like measles, malaria, typhoid fever (caused by dirty water), yellow fever, and diarrhea went through the camps as epidemics. And doctors just didn't know what to do to stop the epidemics.

The third reason, the unclean conditions of the men and the camps, was one that people of the time simply did not realize would cause disease. It is hard to believe, but this was a time when people thought that taking a bath too often could kill you. No one understood the importance of washing hands before eating and other simple actions that everyone today knows can help keep you healthy. Doctors would use medical instruments on one patient, then just go to the next patient and use the same instruments, without even washing them.

Soldiers coming into the army would almost always get sick right away with what we now call the childhood diseases. Most soldiers coming from rural areas might never have been exposed to diseases like measles and mumps as children. Now whole regiments would go through epidemics of these diseases. Unfortunately, these diseases and the complications, like pneumonia, that many people get from them are much worse in adults than in children. The soldiers who survived these epidemics would already be weak when they were exposed to the routine camp diseases like diarrhea and dysentery, which all the soldiers lived with daily.

In reading through the Surgeon General's *Medical and Surgical History of the War of Rebellion* and the report of the U.S. Sanitary Commission, what is amazing, after a while, is not how many men died from disease. It is, rather, how many people did not die, given the terrible conditions in which they lived while fighting during the Civil War. It's even more amazing that anyone could have had the strength and energy left to fight each other at all, considering the level of disease in army camps.

Chapter 5

DYING FROM WOUNDS

Soldiers who were hit by the bullets used during the Civil War tended to be much more severely wounded than those wounded in wars before or after the Civil War. During the Revolutionary War and the War of 1812, soldiers fired muskets with a smooth barrel. These shot a round ball of lead that usually broke the skin and fractured a bone where it lodged. But most soldiers during the Civil War were using a new kind of musket and new ammunition, called Minié balls. These were much more deadly.

The new guns had a rifled barrel, which means that there were spiral grooves cut into the inside of the barrel. The new Minié balls, which were shaped like cones, had special grooves that matched the grooves in the gun barrels. When the rifle was fired, these grooves would cause the Minié ball to spin so that it was going much faster when it left the gun. Rifled muskets also were far more accurate at a much longer range than the old muskets with smooth barrels. When the Minié ball hit something, the top of the cone shape would flatten out, resulting in a more serious injury. Because of its shape and the fact that it was traveling faster, when it hit a person it would usually make a gaping wound with a lot more damage to the bones and the soft tissue and muscles around the bones.

By World War I, the bullets were of steel and didn't flatten out when they hit something. And these bullets traveled at such a high speed that they would usually go right through the person they hit. But Civil War soldiers had the worst of both kinds. Their new bullets traveled faster than the old musket balls, but they were still slow enough that they usually remained inside the body. The result was splintered bones with lots of damage to everything around the bones. That meant that there was a need for more amputations of arms and legs so mangled they could not be saved.

Seven out of every ten soldiers who were hit by rifle fire during the Civil War were hit in the arm or the leg. Two out of the ten were hit in the body itself, and only one out of ten in the head or the face. A whopping 94% of all the Civil War injuries were caused by the new Minié balls or the older style musket balls. Only 6% of the injuries came from the shells or the canisters fired from cannons. And with all the stories one reads about Civil War soldiers fighting in hand-to-hand combat, using swords or bayonets, less than a thousand soldiers were ever injured by a sword or bayonet, and only fifty-six died that way.

The pictures show, better than words can, how much damage was done by the weapons used in the fighting. And the words of the nurses who came to care for the wounded soldiers and who saw these wounds are powerful reminders of what it must have been like to be a wounded soldier during the Civil War.

Hannah L. Palmer, a school teacher from New York, became a Union army nurse. She remembers: "Many of the wounds made at the battle of the Wilderness were of a very painful nature; the balls often striking against trees, and becoming flattened, glanced, and then, entering the flesh, tore their way with ragged edge sometimes leaving in the wounds bits of bark or moss."

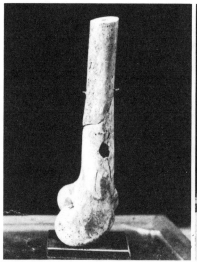
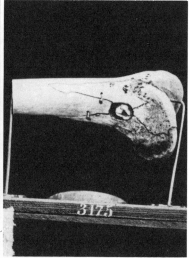
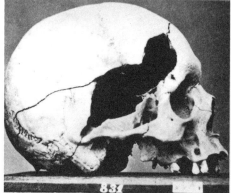
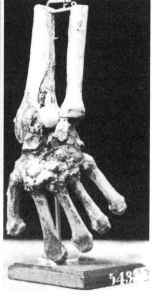

a, b, c, and d. This group of photographs shows the damage done
by Minié balls compared to the
simple injury from a musket ball.
Notice the splintering of the bone
in all but the wrist picture. The
musket ball in the wrist is just
lodged there without doing all the damage done by the Minié
balls in the other pictures. (Photos #PS 3175 (9a); PS 3670
(9b); PS 831 (9c); PS 543 (9d); Otis Historical Archives,
National Museum of Health and Medicine, Armed Forces
Institute of Pathology.)

Private John A. Howard, of a Pennsylvania cavalry unit, was cut by a saber, which fractured his skull during a skirmish at Amelia Court House, Virginia on April 5, 1865. There were actually very few sword or saber injuries during the Civil War. (Photo #CP 915, Otis Historical Archives, National Museum of Health and Medicine, Armed Forces Institute of Pathology.)

Private Frederick A. Bentley, of the 185th New York Regiment, received this gunshot wound in his chest in a skirmish at Stone Creek, Virginia on March 29, 1865. (Photo #CP 1016, Otis Historical Archives, National Museum of Health and Medicine, Armed Forces Institute of Pathology.)

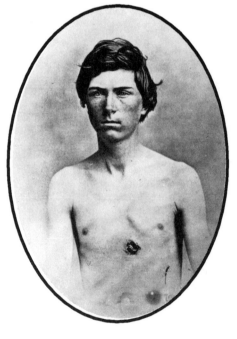

This close-up picture of a gunshot fracture of the lower leg bone of Private William Rodenbaugh, of Pennsylvania, shows the splintering of the bone where the ball entered. The leg had to be amputated. (Photo #CP 1252, Otis Historical Archives, National Museum of Health and Medicine, Armed Forces Institute of Pathology.)

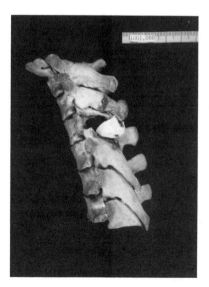

This picture shows part of the backbone of a twenty-two-year-old Confederate soldier from Georgia who was injured in the fighting near Washington, DC on July 14, 1864. He died the next day. Notice the Minié ball that made the wound. (Otis Historical Archives, National Museum of Health and Medicine, Armed Forces Institute of Pathology.)

Nurse Sophronia E. Bucklin describes what a battle-field looked like just after a battle: "I visited the battle ground on several occasions — the first time soon after the conflict, when the evidence of the horrid carnage which had ranged over it, lay on every hand in fearful sights. Shells had fallen without exploding, tempting some of the curious and heedless to their destruction ... Battered canteens, cartridge-boxes, torn knapsacks, muskets twisted by cannon shot and shell, rusted tin cups, pieces of rent uniform, caps, belts perforated with shot, and heaps of death's leaden hail, marked the spots where men were stricken down in solid ranks."

William Howell Reed in his memoir says: "The sights of a field of carnage must not be described. But in the rear of it we can see men sitting under trees, or lying in agony, having crawled to some shady spot to a brook-side or ravine where they may bathe their fevered wounds or quench their thirst, while waiting their turn to be removed in ambulances to the hospital."

Chapter 6

PEOPLE OF MEDICINE —
SURGEONS AND STEWARDS

However brilliant the tactics and strategy, it should be remembered that an essential factor in all warfare must be the physical efficiency of the man behind the gun ... It should not be forgotten that it is only through the unwearying and unobtrusive efforts of the surgeons that men and armies are kept in fighting trim. Not surprisingly, these words were written by an army surgeon, Dr. Edward L. Munson.

The job of a surgeon during the Civil War was not an easy one. He (or she, because there were a few women surgeons) had to care for his patients under dangerous conditions without the proper supplies. The surgeon, who was not allowed to carry a gun, was often under fire while treating his patients. He was also chancing death from all the diseases he was treating. Because there were so few, a surgeon had to work long hours, particularly after major battles. Many of the soldiers hated him. When he walked into the room, some soldiers reached for their guns, in fear that he had come to amputate some part of their body. He probably felt he was doing his job well and that over time he would be appreciated for his effort and self-sacrifice. But even this was not to be so. History has called him a "butcher" and laughed at his ignorance and lack of knowledge. None of it is fair to

Surgeons and hospital stewards pose outside one of the Union hospitals in Washington, DC. Note how much cleaner they and their surroundings are compared with General Kearny's Brigade Hospital staff. (National Library of Medicine.)

Union General Kearny's Brigade Hospital with the staff posing in front. (National Library of Medicine.)

a group of people who gave their time and sometimes their lives to help the sick and wounded soldiers of the Civil War.

When the Civil War started, the Union Army's medical forces had only 115 doctors in its ranks — a surgeon-general, thirty surgeons, and eighty-four assistant surgeons. To make things worse, twenty-seven of these medical personnel left the army and returned to their Southern homeland. By the end of the long war, over 13,000 doctors had served in the Union Army. They treated over 5,825,000 individual cases of wounds or disease. Thirty-two surgeons died in battle. Eighty-three were wounded in battle, ten of these later died, and 281 died from the various diseases common to the army. The Confederate Army was served by 3,500 surgeons.

The Civil War also saw the first service of female doctors. The first woman who graduated from medical school in the U.S., Elizabeth Blackwell, had finished her studies in 1849, only twelve years before the Civil War began. It was natural that some of these new women doctors would want to care for the sick and wounded soldiers. Mary Edwards Walker from New York is probably the best remembered woman doctor in the war. Her pocket medical kit is part of the collection at the National Museum of Health and Medicine in Washington. She found that the male medical leadership was not happy to accept female surgeons. Mary Walker served three years as a nurse in the Civil War and only became an assistant surgeon in her fourth year of service.

Esther Hill Hawks, another woman doctor who wished to serve the troops along with her doctor-husband, was repeatedly refused. Dorothea Dix, the head of Union Army nurses, would not even allow her to serve as a nurse because she was young and attractive. She eventually was allowed to practice medicine caring for the wounded soldiers of the 54th Massachusetts Infantry, a unit of black soldiers. For most of the Civil War, however, she was only allowed to be a teacher in a school for freed slaves. With the army desperate for surgeons, it seems a shame that they would waste the services of the women doctors who wanted to help.

At the beginning of the Civil War, surgeons could be captured by either side and imprisoned. The idea that the medical staff shouldn't be shot at and captured because they were not participating in the fighting had never occurred to anyone. This "neutral" status that we take for granted in modern warfare did not exist at the beginning of the Civil War. It was not until May 1862, during a battle at Winchester, Virginia, that Confederate General "Stonewall" Jackson established a new policy that would become one of the "rules" of modern warfare. He had captured a Federal hospital and he returned the staff to their own army because he felt, in the words of Dr. Munson, "that as the surgeons did not make war they should not suffer its penalties." Now at least the surgeons could care for their patients close to the front lines without having to protect themselves from capture.

The system set up for medical care on both sides in the Civil War looked great on paper. But in practice, getting materials to the surgeons and arranging for the space the surgeons needed to do their job did not work out as it was planned. With armies on the march, it was hard to keep their supplies with them. Realistically, the army leadership wanted to make sure that ammunition got to the soldiers first. Their second priority was food, and the memoirs left by many soldiers showed that food often did not get to the soldiers for quite a while. Medical supplies only came third on the list.

Smart surgeons learned to carry with them what they would need without relying on supply wagons. A surgeon would carry his instruments with him in his "surgeon's field companion" and his orderly would carry a "hospital knapsack" that weighed about twenty pounds. The rest of the things he needed he would have to come up with from local materials or other available army supplies. Thus, surgery in the field was often done with the patient lying on a board stretched between two barrels. A door from a nearby house was frequently used as an operating table — if one was available. Because bandages were bulky to carry, the surgeon would make do, reusing the same bandage on other patients. Reading about conditions under which field surgeons worked, it is much easier to understand why so many soldiers died.

Doctors at the general hospitals had somewhat better conditions in which to work. But they also had patients who, by the time they arrived at the general hospital, were already sick and weak. Story after story tells of the horrible conditions at these hospitals. In fact, the U.S. Sanitary Commission was set up by people who were concerned about the treatment of the Civil War soldiers and who wanted to make sure that the army was providing good medical care. The reports of the Sanitary Commission inspectors, especially during the early part of the war, describe only nightmare conditions. But knowing that they were being watched, the army medical leadership improved conditions later in the war.

Part of the problem for surgeons in charge of hospital facilities was that their time was wasted on tasks that could have been done by some other officer. One memoir by a Confederate surgeon, Dr. Deering J. Roberts, talks of being assigned to set up a hospital in December 1864 in Tennessee. He was given the service of a hospital steward, ten soldiers on detail to assist him, and two wagons. He then describes the whole process and almost all of it is administrative work. He selects buildings to use, arranges to have them cleaned out, negotiates for carpenters to construct bunks, travels into the countryside to find clean straw. All this administrative work had to be done before he could begin to care for any patients.

Memoirs by nurses and Sanitary Commission volunteers routinely blame surgeons for the poor hospital conditions. Confederate nurse Kate Cumming, arriving at a new hospital, records in her diary, "The amount of good done is not near what it might be, if things were better managed. Someone is to blame for this state of affairs. Many say that it is the fault of Dr. Foard, the medical director."

Army doctors really had only one assistant assigned to them under army regulations, their hospital steward. Unlike surgeons, who were officers, the stewards were non-commissioned officers with the rank of sergeant. The steward assisted the surgeon with some of the administrative details. But his most important job was as pharmacist for the hospital. The steward was in charge of all the medicine used by the doctors. He was also responsible for all the dressing (bandaging) of wounds and for keeping the hospital clean. In the Union Army, where dentists were not used, he also acted as dentist for the unit.

Between them, surgeons and stewards were responsible for the medical care of everyone assigned to them as well as for the administration of the hospital. They were the persons that the army leadership recognized as the medical staff for the soldiers. Others helped them, as we will see, but they were the "official" medical staff of the army when the Civil War began.

Chapter 7

PEOPLE OF MEDICINE — NURSES AND OTHER STAFF

In the military hierarchy, surgeons and stewards were supposed to be able to provide all the care necessary to wounded and sick soldiers. But very early in the Civil War it became obvious that this was not going to be like any other war the American army had been involved in. This war, with its massive number of people, was going to need a more efficient medical care system. In the first year of the war, the medical corps just struggled along, doing the best they could. Finally, in September 1862, Congress passed a law to provide better care for the wounded and sick soldiers. General hospitals were established. These, in addition to the stewards and surgeons, would be staffed with matrons, assistant matrons, ward matrons, nurses, cooks, laundresses, and other workers as needed.

Each general hospital would have two matrons. Their job was to be in charge of getting food for the patients. There were also two assistant matrons, to take charge of the hospital laundry and be responsible for clothing for the patients. The ward matrons, two for each hundred patients, had to keep the ward beds ready and the ward clean. They also made sure that patients received their food and medicine and that they got the care needed. All matrons were mostly administrators, supervising the people who actually did the cleaning, cooking, and washing of the bed linens and the clothing.

The final group of hospital staff authorized were the nurses. When the Civil War began, nursing was done by Catholic or Protestant nuns, the only trained nurses in the country. They became the first nurses to serve in general hospitals during the Civil War. The other source of "nurses" was the relatives of soldiers who were wounded in battle. Family members who were able came to nurse their soldier through his convalescence. Often they were willing to help out nursing other patients in the same ward. But there remained a need to bring in more nurses. A famous social reformer, Dorothea Dix, offered to serve as Superintendent of Nurses for the Army as a volunteer. Her offer was accepted. She became one of the most important persons in the army, determining who would be military nurses and what their duties would be.

Dorothea Dix had very definite views on who would make a suitable nurse. According to her standards, in order to become a nurse a woman had to be over thirty years old and healthy. She had to be very plain looking and dress in brown or black. She couldn't wear hoop skirts or bows on her dresses. She couldn't have curled hair or wear jewelry. These rules angered many women who wanted to serve as nurses. But Miss Dix was very strict about her requirements and rejected many women who wished to help. Some women got around Miss Dix's requirements by applying directly to the Surgeon General and getting assigned to a hospital by him. But, for the most part, Dorothea Dix remained in charge of all nursing staff for the Union hospitals during the Civil War. Her views on the limited amount of work that could be done by the nurses and on the proper image of a nurse matched those of the military leadership. Some

A Sanitary Commission nurse with her patients at a hospital in Fredericksburg, Virginia in May 1864. (National Library of Medicine.)

people, looking back on the Civil War, criticize her strict views. But in terms of what women were usually allowed to do at the time, she was really giving them new duties and responsibilities that would not have seemed possible before the war began.

Nurses during the Civil War did not work in field hospitals. They served only in the general hospitals far back from the lines. There were a few exceptions to this among the three to four thousand nurses who served in the Civil War. One was Clara Barton. Miss Barton was not going to let anyone keep her away from the battlefield. She traveled to the field in her own wagon loaded with supplies. Another was "Mother" Bickerdyke, who

Clara Barton, the "Angel of the Battlefield," traveled to battlefields in her own wagon stocked with medical supplies. Most nurses were only allowed to serve in general hospitals. Miss Barton was one of the few who tended soldiers in the field. (National Library of Medicine.)

Social reformer Dorothea Dix volunteered to organize nursing services for the Union army. She had very strict rules for her nurses, including that they be over thirty, dress in black or brown, and not have curled hair. (National Library of Medicine.)

was a member of the Sanitary Commission and helped out in the West. She supposedly was on the scene of nineteen separate battles, nursing the soldiers right on the field where they fell. One Southern nurse also became very famous. Sally Tompkins opened a hospital in Richmond in 1862 and paid all the expenses to keep it running until the end of the war. For her work she was named a captain in the Confederate army. She was the only female Confederate officer appointed during the war.

Most of the nurses who served in the Civil War had more routine duties. They changed dressings, gave out medicine, washed patients, and also did things that we don't think of as being nursing duties today. Nurses during the Civil War cooked food for their patients, read and sang to them, wrote letters for them, and prayed with them. For all this work, nurses on both sides received a salary of eleven dollars a month.

Helping out with the care of the patients were the members of the Sanitary Commission, which was formed in the early part of the war. Their original mission had been to inspect what the medical leadership was doing and make recommendations to the political leaders to ensure the soldiers received good care. Their second mission was to provide items that the army could not provide for the soldiers who were sick or wounded. The Sanitary Commission assisted directly with sending nurses to hospitals that needed them. They also opened and ran forty Soldiers' Homes for soldiers on their way to or from the battlefield who didn't have money to stay in other places. They worked to have a hospital directory in place so that people could track down patients in any of the 243 general army hospitals. They set up a "Claim Agency" to help soldiers get their pay and pension benefits. They organized supply wagons for "Battle-Field Relief."

Mary Livermore, who was very active in Sanitary Commission work in Chicago, said that after the battle of Antietam, the "Battle-Field Relief" wagons distributed "28,763 pieces of dry goods, shirts, towels, bed-ticks, pillows, etc.; 30 barrels of old linen, bandages, and lint; 3,188 pounds of farina [oat cereal]; 2,260 pounds of condensed milk; 5,000 pounds of beefstock and canned meats; 3,000 bottles of wine and cordials; 4,000 sets of hospital clothing; several tons of lemons and other fruit; crackers, tea, sugar, rubber cloth, tin cups, chloroform, opiates, surgical instruments, and other 'hospital' conveniences." All this was given for just one battle for the care of 10,000 wounded soldiers. She goes on to give numbers for other battles where the Sanitary Commission was involved. All this material was "free," collected from donations from over ten thousand soldiers' aid societies set up in the north during the war.

For many Civil War nurses, time spent in hospitals caring for the soldiers would be remembered as one of the most important events in their lives. The hundreds of memoirs written by former nurses provide a human perspective on the suffering of the soldiers that doesn't always come through in the memoirs of the doctors. Sanitary Commission member Mary Livermore remembers: "It was a sad sight to pass through the wards and see row after row of narrow beds, with white, worn, still faces pressed against the white pillows. And it gave one a heartache to take each man by the hand and listen to his simple story, and to hear his anxieties for wife and children."

Confederate nurse Kate Cumming remembered caring for some Union prisoners this way: "Seeing an enemy wounded and helpless is a different thing from seeing him in health and in power. The first time I saw one in this condition every feeling of enmity vanished at once."

She writes later in her diary of finding a soldier who had died during the night with no one noticing: "These are terrible things, and, what is more heart-rending, no one seems to mind them."

Union nurse Sophronia E. Bucklin writes of people trying to discourage her from going off as a nurse. "'It is no place for women' was the cry on every hand. Hospitals were as the house of death, in the mind of respectable and virtuous communities." But their feelings did not stop her: "With the picture of horror-strewn slaughter-ground laid vividly before me; with the well-wrought details of hospital suffering brought to my mind in strong truthful colors; with sickness and possible death made plain to my vision ... I said, 'If any woman has done this, I can.'"

Army nurse Amanda Colburn Farnham, who became a nurse so that she could follow after her brother who enlisted in the Third Vermont Regiment, would always remember an occasion where she was more than just a nurse. Two days after the Battle of Antietam, she was helping to care for the wounded. She came upon a boy who had been shot in the chest but still had not been seen by the surgeons. Her husband's account of what she did, written after her death, states: "Taking the only implement she had, a pair of sharp button-hole scissors, and pinching the ball with her thumb and finger, she made a slight incision and pressed the ball out." He says that she "was one of Miss Dix's trusted nurses, and was charged with duties and commissions at the front that she would trust to no one else."

The nurses' stories go on and on. These are only a few examples of what they saw and how they did their jobs under very trying conditions during the Civil War — for many, the most memorable event of their lives.

Chapter 8

TRANSPORTATION FROM BATTLEFIELD TO HOSPITAL

The U.S. Army bought their first ambulances only a couple of years before the Civil War began. In the first big battle of the Civil War, the ambulances were driven by civilian drivers. In the panic of the fighting and the Union defeat, the ambulance drivers got scared and fled to Washington, leaving the wounded to get back to hospitals as best they could on their own. It was a horrible disaster. But it made clear to the military leaders that something had to be done about transporting the wounded soldiers from the battlefield to field hospitals, and on to regimental hospitals and later to general hospitals.

The ambulance corps finally got its official start in August 1862 with its own rules and specific equipment for transport. Each regiment would have a transport cart, a four-wheel ambulance, and two two-wheel ambulances. There would be two stretchers for each ambulance and two men and a driver to move the sick. The ambulances must have been terribly painful places, especially for men with untreated wounds. There were all kinds of ambulances but none of them was very comfortable. Many didn't even have springs, so the wounded soldiers were bounced around for the entire ride. The two-wheel ambulances did more than bounce their patients. The soldiers nicknamed them "avalanches" because they were so unstable that the patients tended to slide right out of them.

William Howell Reed helped transport the wounded after the battle of Fredericksburg, and described the nightmare of ambulance transport this way: "On the ambulances are concentrated probably more acute suffering than may be seen in the same space in all the world beside. The worst cases only have the privilege of transportation ... A privilege of being violently tossed from side to side, of having one of the four who occupy the vehicle together thrown bodily, perhaps, upon a gaping wound; of being tortured, and racked, and jolted, when each jarring of the ambulance is enough to make the sympathetic brain burst with agony."

Soldiers wounded in battle were carried on stretchers to the field hospital. From there the ambulances transported them to the regimental hospitals. After their conditions were stablized, they were transported on special railroad cars or hospital ships to the big general hospitals. The train cars at times were only unheated cattle cars, but as the war went on, special cars with beds, kitchens, and actual surgeries were available for transport. Over time, the system worked so well that after the battle of Gettysburg, when 20,000 wounded were left behind, over 15,000 of them were transferred to general hospitals in Baltimore, York, Harrisburg, and New York City within two weeks, all by railroad.

Hospital ships were used for transport of wounded soldiers on the Mississippi River and along the east coast. One ship, the U.S. Hospital Steamer *Charles McDougall*, was able to transport 12,299 sick and wounded soldiers in five months' time. Frederick Law Olmsted, secretary of the Sanitary Commission, wrote a memoir of the "Floating Hospital Service" from Virginia in 1862. Here he was able to capture the fast, frantic pace of working on a hospital ship. He talks of the tugs swarming around the ship trying to get their patients loaded on before the ship is too full. He writes of desperately trying to find supplies and getting things ready between loads of patients. His responsibility was providing food for the patients, and he shares his frustration at trying to get his job done "at short notice, in confined space, and with the aid of very limited cooking facilities." And he managed to give a feeling for what chaos there must have been as he writes: "After a battle, when men are brought in so rapidly that they have to be piled in almost without reference to their being human beings, and everyone raving for drink first and then nourishment, it requires strong nerves to be able to attend to them properly."

Members of the Ambulance Corps load soldiers into an ambulance at a field hospital. (National Library of Medicine.)

The U.S. Hospital Ship Red Rover. Hospital ships were used to move patients along the east coast and on the Mississippi River. (National Library of Medicine.)

This is a model of a hospital train car that is part of an exhibit at the National Museum of Health and Medicine. It is constructed to look like the cars used for transporting patients in the Union army in 1863. (Historical Collections, National Museum of Health and Medicine, Armed Forces Institute of Pathology.)

Chapter 9

HOSPITALS

When the Civil War began in 1861, the biggest military hospitals had only forty beds. By the time the war ended, the Confederate Army had built the largest general military hospital ever in Richmond. It had eight thousand beds arranged in five separate hospitals. Each separate hospital was made up of thirty buildings, each holding forty to sixty patients. The one-story buildings, 30 feet by 100 feet, were joined by five soup houses, five icehouses, a bathhouse, a brewery, and a bakery big enough to make ten thousand loaves of bread a day. Chimborazo Hospital also included its own farm to produce food to be used by the patients. Between the beginning and the end of the Civil War, there had been a revolutionary change in the whole idea of military hospitals and their role in the care of soldiers in wartime.

At the beginning of the Civil War, it was an accepted belief of military leaders throughout the world that military hospitals should be small, regimental-size units. There was even a medical reason for this belief. The death rate during the Crimean War in Europe had been terribly high. Doctors decided that the reason for this was the large, crowded hospitals where soldiers were exposed to all the other sick soldiers. Since most hospitals were filthy, smelly places, this was not at all a bad theory.

This painting shows the U.S. Capitol being used as a hospital in the early part of the Civil War. Government buildings were used to house wounded soldiers after the first battle at Manassas. (National Library of Medicine.)

Some of the 150 buildings that made up Chimborazo Hospital in Richmond, the largest military hospital ever built, with beds for 8,000 patients. (National Library of Medicine.)

What the army leaders were not prepared for was the number of injuries there would be and how many of the soldiers would require long-term care. They also did not plan on the disease rate that sent so many soldiers to the hospitals. Most important of all, they thought the Civil War was going to be a fairly brief war, with perhaps one major battle. No one anticipated that it would end up as a four-year ordeal. Everyone was surprised how long the war lasted. The length of the war meant the military planning for things like medical care was unrealistic. As the care of the soldiers fell apart in the weeks after the first battle at Manassas (Bull Run), many concerned people realized that changes in the system would have to be made. But the military was still too busy trying to get ready to fight a long war and the leadership just didn't have time to worry about medical care. Thus, the U.S. Sanitary Commission was formed as an inspection agency to act for the soldiers, whom it felt the army leaders were neglecting. The creation of the Sanitary Commission was not popular with the military and political leaders. Even President Lincoln called it a "fifth wheel" and at first thought it wasn't necessary. But its people did get the system to change.

While waiting for buildings to be built to house the sick and wounded soldiers, both the Union and the Confederacy turned their capital cities into giant hospitals. In Richmond, church pews served as hospital beds. In Washington, a hospital was set up in the Rotunda of the Capitol. Confederate General Robert E. Lee's home in Arlington, which was in Union hands, was converted into a hospital.

At the same time, an incredible building project began. By early 1863, the Union had over 150 hospitals ready. By the end of the war, there were over 135,000 beds available in hospitals across Union territory. The

Confederates were busy with the same kinds of projects, leading to the largest hospital ever, Chimborazo, described earlier. The Confederate government chose to build fewer hospitals but to make them much larger. The Union leaders spread theirs out throughout the north but tended to build mostly smaller, 500-bed hospitals.

Most of the hospitals were built in what was called pavilion style. This meant that they were usually only one or two stories high with wards isolated from each other. Sometimes each ward was a separate building, as at Chimborazo. At other times a series of pavilions was built coming off a center section where kitchens and laundries were located. The pavilion style was copied from one that was used by the British in the Crimean War. This arrangement allowed for better ventilation, and all the medical books of the time kept talking about the need for good ventilation in hospitals. This is because doctors thought diseases were transmitted by "bad" air. The system worked well. In getting rid of "bad" air, the hospital designers were really helping rid the wards of the viruses that are passed by sneezing and coughing people living in crowded, closed rooms.

More important for the patients' health, the new hospitals were planned with improved sanitation systems for disposing of waste materials. Although it was hard to get the soldiers to use the system, it did help to cut down on diseases caused by dirty drinking water contaminated by human waste.

As the war went on, the memoirs of people who visited or worked in the hospitals began to have positive things to say about hospital conditions. Confederate nurse Kate Cumming, who had described some shocking conditions at army hospitals, saw improvements at others: "Dr. Smith has taken charge of this hospital. I

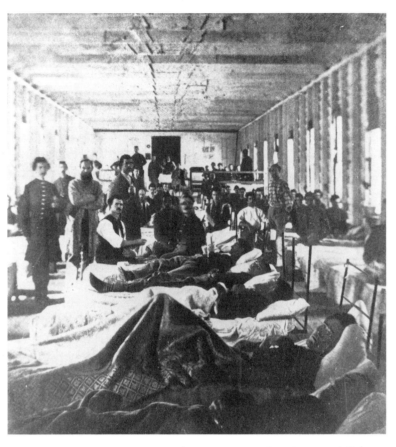

A crowded ward at a convalescent camp for Union soldiers in Alexandria, Virginia. (National Library of Medicine.)

think there will be a different order of things now. He is having the house and yard well cleansed. Before this, it was common to have amputated limbs thrown into the yard, and left there." Mary Livermore, a Union Sanitary Commission nurse, contrasts a general hospital with some horrible ones she had seen earlier: "Here were order, comfort, cleanliness, and good nursing. The food was cooked in a kitchen outside the hospital. Surgeons were detailed to every ward, who visited their patients twice daily ... The apothecary's room was supplied with an ample store of medicines and surgical appliances, and the store-room possessed an abundance of clothing and delicacies for the sick."

The military hospital system had come a long way from the chaos after Manassas. Especially in the general hospitals, wounded and sick soldiers were receiving better care in cleaner conditions than at the beginning of the war. Some of the hospitals could even brag of very low death rates for their patients. The Civil War had led to changes in hospitals that would help to make health care better for all Americans, not just soldiers, in the years after the Civil War.

Chapter 10

THE WOUNDED SOLDIER: FIELD HOSPITAL TO GENERAL HOSPITAL

As the army made plans to go into battle, the surgeons would be told to set up their field hospitals. They would select a place close to the battle area but about two miles or so behind the lines. They needed to be close for transport but not so close that they could be hit by cannon fire. First choice for location would be some sort of a building like a church or house or barn. But if one wasn't available, tents could always be set up. The commander of the regiment would then detail men to serve as "nurses" and stretcher carriers for the surgeons during the battle and to help get everything ready for the battle casualties. These might be members of the regimental band or people on "light" duty who were unable to fight. Several books say that the commanders usually picked their "shirkers" whom they felt might try to get out of the fighting anyway.

Once the field hospital was set up, the assistant surgeons and their orderlies would set up "primary" stations right behind the battle lines. These were like first-aid stations. Doctors and other medical people on the front lines wore special badges so that, with luck, no one would fire at them while they worked so close to the fighting. They were also not allowed to carry guns. The soldier "nurses" or medics detailed from the unit would

57

Wounded soldiers outside a field hospital near the battlefield in Fredericksburg, Virginia. (National Library of Medicine.)

Soldiers wounded at Gettysburg are in tents near the Second Corps Hospital in 1863. (National Library of Medicine.)

One of the new large general military hospitals in Washington, DC. (National Library of Medicine.)

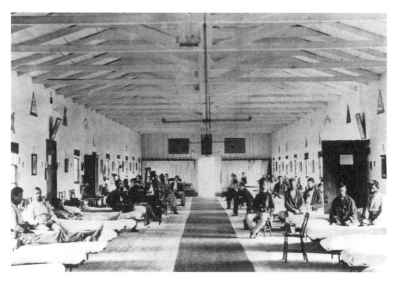

U.S. Army hospital at Armory Square in Washington, DC. This one is much less crowded than the Alexandria convalescent camp. (National Library of Medicine.)

be the only ones who could go to help the wounded and bring them back to the primary station. The rules were very strict that no fighting soldiers were allowed to stop fighting to help someone who had been shot.

As the fighting started, men who had received minor wounds would walk to the primary station for help. Soldiers who were badly wounded would be carried on stretchers back to the primary station by medics. There the assistant surgeons would give them emergency first aid. They would try to stop the bleeding, quickly bandage the wounds, and give them medicine, for pain, and whiskey, which they thought would prevent the wounded soldier from going into shock. That was all they really could do at a primary station right on the front lines. Patients were then sent back to the field hospitals. Those who were able to walk had to walk the two miles on their own. The badly wounded were brought there in ambulances.

The surgeons at the field hospital were waiting for them. Here was where the decision would be made on whether an amputation was needed. All the emergency (or primary) operations were done right here, only a mile or two behind the lines. Patients were then sent on to general hospitals a few days after the battle, to complete their recovery. Many of the wounded who were going to die died within the first few days and never left the field hospitals.

The field hospital surgeons had to take care of anyone brought into their hospital. At the first big battle of the Civil War, Manassas, many regimental surgeons refused to care for wounded who were not from their own regiments. That meant that some field hospitals were swamped with patients while others had nothing to do. After Manassas, orders were given that all surgeons had to treat all soldiers to prevent that from ever happening again.

The field hospitals were the weakest part of the whole medical system. Because they were set up at the last moment and because their supplies often didn't catch up with them, these were the places most likely to be dirty and deadly. The field hospitals, or the regimental hospitals when the soldiers were in camp, had a terrible reputation that did not seem to improve as the war went on. In spite of this reputation, many soldiers did not want to be transferred from their own field hospitals when they were sick or wounded, because they thought they would get better care with people they knew. But in fact, they stood a much better chance of surviving if they were sent to a general hospital, especially in the last half of the war. Mary Livermore describes conditions at a regimental hospital she visited: "Were I to describe them as I saw them, the account would be discredited. Compressed with their narrow limits were more filth and discomfort, neglect and suffering, ... The fetid odor of typhoid fever ... was rendered more nauseating by unclean beds and unwashed bodies."

Part of the problem at these hospitals is that they never had the help of nurses, matrons, and Sanitary Commission people to keep them clean. The field and regimental hospitals were staffed by surgeons and "nurses" who were soldiers recuperating from being sick or wounded themselves. Unless family members came to help out, these hospitals just didn't have the people available to provide good nursing care to the soldiers.

Fortunately, the sickest patients and the badly wounded were transferred to the general hospitals to recover. Confederate nurse Kate Cumming wrote in her diary of a visit from a doctor who was caring for fifty wounded men but had no supplies with which to feed them. Her record of what he told her would have been good advice for the medical leadership planning patient

An abandoned Confederate field hospital near Petersburg, Virginia, captured by Union troops on June 15, 1864. (National Library of Medicine.)

care on both sides of the war: "He said that if our men were not better treated than at the present time, it would be the means of demoralizing them more than the enemy's balls."

Chapter 11

MEDICAL INSTRUMENTS

Many of the instruments found in the Civil War surgeon's medical kit look as if they belong in someone's tool kit. But each of the items the surgeons carried was necessary for the kind of surgery they were doing most of the time. Every surgeon in the Union Army was given five cases of instruments to use, what Doctor Samuel Gross called their "armamentarium." Surgeons were responsible for keeping track of their instruments and for returning them at the end of their service. They received an amputating case, a trephining set for head surgery, an exsecting case, a general operating kit, and a pocket medical kit. They were also given a leather trunk and a three-month supply of eighty different medicines.

Included in this chapter are pictures of a surgeon's kit owned by Dr. Stephen Pierson of Orange, New Jersey. It is part of the collection at the National Museum of Health and Medicine at Walter Reed Army Hospital in Washington, DC. This is a standard surgeon's kit that was given to each Union Army surgeon during the Civil War for use in battle.

The instruments in the kit are all very functional and would be used continually by the surgeon in the field and at the field and regimental hospitals. There are the amputating knives and saws for cutting off arms and

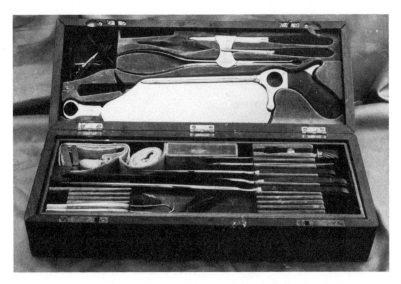

U.S. Army surgical kit belonging to Dr. Stephen Pierson, of Orange, New Jersey. (Historical Collections, National Museum of Health and Medicine, Armed Forces Institute of Pathology.)

Amputating instruments from Dr. Pierson's kit, including saws and a tourniquet for controlling bleeding. (Historical Collections, National Museum of Health and Medicine, Armed Forces Institute of Pathology.)

Forceps used to remove bullets from wounds. These are also from Dr. Pierson's kit. (Historical Collections, National Museum of Health and Medicine, Armed Forces Institute of Pathology.)

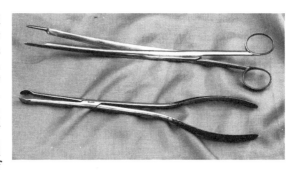

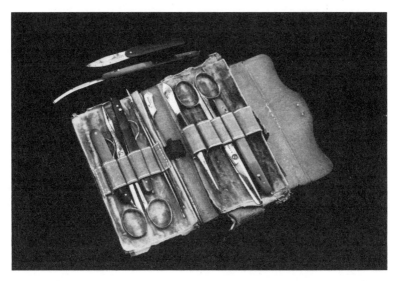

Dr. Mary Walker's pocket medical kit was used in battlefield first aid stations where only very basic techniques were attempted before sending the wounded back to the field hospitals. (Historical Collections, National Museum of Health and Medicine, Armed Forces Institute of Pathology.)

legs too badly wounded to be saved. Especially in the early part of the Civil War, amputation was the treatment recommended to doctors if they wanted to save the patient's life. There is also the tourniquet used to stop the bleeding so the amputation could be done. Tools were included for doing surgery on the head, including a trephine, which was used to drill a hole in the skull to relieve pressure on the brain. There are scalpels and forceps used for cutting tissue and removing bullets.

Many times the doctor working right on the field wouldn't even bother with a kit this large. He would save that kit for working in the field hospital. Instead he (or she, because the pocket kit pictured in this chapter belonged to U.S. surgeon Mary Walker) would carry a small pocket medical kit for quick work on the field.

To go with the surgical kit, the doctors also carried medicine cases to hold their medicines and their chloroform for anesthesia. Many of the cases also held all the things the surgeons would need for bandaging the soldiers' wounds.

Army surgeon Edward L. Munson knew what it was like to actually use these materials in the field. He writes about all the equipment and how he and his orderly had to transport it. He talks about the lack of necessary things like bandages, and of soldiers covering wounds with "a dirty handkerchief or piece of cloth torn from a sweaty shirt." He writes of the lack of needed medicines. He complains of how many of the needed materials were transported by the wagons and weren't where the surgeon needed them after a battle. And he talks of routinely using instruments "without more than superficial cleansing ... with the result that they habitually conveyed infection." He writes of surgeons operating under fire while the battle was still going on "under conditions in which even the pretense of surgical cleanliness could not have been maintained."

Chapter 12

SURGERY

People of today looking back on the work of Civil War surgeons often think of them as butchers. During the Civil War, in the Union Army three out of every four operations were amputations. More arms and legs were cut off during the Civil War than in any other war in our history. In fact, the picture in most people's minds of Civil War medicine is the image of piles of arms and legs thrown aside after amputation.

Doctors had good sound medical reasons for amputating so many arms and legs. Part of their decision came from the damage done by the new Minié balls shot from rifled gun barrels. These did more harm to tissue around the splintered bone and led to more infections after the injury. Part of it was that the medical statistics really did show that a soldier stood a better chance of surviving if his gunshot arm or leg was amputated. One doctor, presenting his research on whether to amputate right after an injury or to wait a couple of days to see what developed, showed that in nineteen cases of primary (immediate) amputation, he was able to save all nineteen patients. But in nineteen cases of secondary (done two days or more after the injury) amputation, only one of the patients survived. With those kinds of numbers, it is not surprising that most surgeons favored immediate amputation of badly wounded arms or legs.

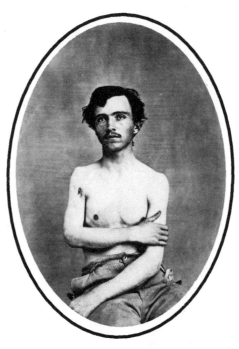

Private William A. Tucker, of Ohio, was wounded at Stone River, Tennessee on April 15, 1863. Instead of amputating, the surgeon used the new operation called an excision, or resection. With three inches of damaged bone removed from his arm, it was shorter but still usable. (Photo #CP 1027, Otis Historical Archives, National Museum of Health and Medicine, Armed Forces Institute of Pathology.)

Private John Cleghorn, of New Jersey, twenty-seven years old, was injured in the fighting at Mine Run, Virginia in November 1863. His first excision operation was not successful. After his second operation, he recovered quickly. (Photo #SP 148, Otis Historical Archives, National Museum of Health and Medicine, Armed Forces Institute of Pathology.)

A new approach to treating these types of wounds was developed during the Civil War. Military surgeons started using a technique called resection, or exsection. In this surgery, they cut away the damaged part of the bone in the arm or leg and reconnected it. This made the arm or leg shorter, but often the procedure could save the arm or leg and leave it still usable by the patient.

Frank Hamilton, the author of a famous military surgery textbook of the time, said almost nothing about resection in the 1861 edition of his book. By the time he wrote the updated edition in 1865, he had a whole chapter devoted to the new procedure, saying that "Exsection, or resection of bones, ... has assumed its chief importance only within the last few years. At the present moment, regarded as a substitution for amputation it is believed to be a positive advance in conservative surgery." He calls resections for the arms "highly satisfactory." Resections for the legs, he admits, are nowhere near as successful but he does note that "as compared with amputations, the results of exsection have thus far proved sufficiently satisfactory in many cases to warrant the continuance of the practice."

No matter whether the surgeons chose amputation or resection, they had very careful guidelines to follow to make their decisions. All the medical texts seem to use the same criteria for deciding whether amputation was needed. Doctors were to look at whether there was just a simple fracture or whether the bone was shattered with damage to other tissues and muscles; whether the main blood supply lines or nerves had been damaged; and whether a joint like the knee was part of the wound. One doctor writes that "Gunshot wounds of the knee-joint are one of the most dangerous of accidents and no attempts should be made to save the limb when the injury is at all extensive." If not, he says "the patient often perishes within the first three or four days."

Amputation was the most horrible part of Civil War medicine. Many soldiers would have rather died than have an arm or a leg amputated. Many stories exist of soldiers who kept their guns and threatened to shoot anyone who tried to amputate one of their arms or legs. Many of those soldiers died without surgery. But many others did survive. Whatever the choice, amputation was everyone's nightmare. Listen as Confederate nurse Kate Cumming describes amputation at the hospital where she was matron: "A stream of blood ran from the table into a tub in which was the arm. It had been taken off at the socket, and the hand, which but a short time before grasped the musket and battled for the right, was hanging over the edge of the tub, a lifeless thing."

Chapter 13

ANESTHESIA

nesthesia was a new development in medicine in the United States before the Civil War. Not much surgery was done at the time and when it was, most of it was done without using anything to deaden the pain. Patients were given lots of whiskey, to prevent "shock," and something hard to bite on (which is where our expression "to bite the bullet" comes from), and that was it.

Doctors knew about anesthesia. It was first demonstrated in the U.S. back in 1846. But since very little surgery was ever done, it was not widely used. The Civil War would give anesthesia its first real test. The Surgeon General's report on the Civil War says anesthesia was used at least 80,000 times during Civil War surgery. Over three quarters of the uses were with chloroform alone. The rest were with ether or ether and chloroform together. The surgeons preferred to use chloroform because ether could catch fire very easily.

A piece of cloth or paper was folded to make a cone with a small piece of sponge in the point of the cone. The chloroform was put on the sponge and the cone was held away from the patient's face and brought gradually closer and closer as the patient breathed, until he was asleep. It was a very safe anesthesia with only forty-three deaths from the anesthesia for the whole war. One Confederate surgeon, Dr. Hunter McGuire, recorded

71

fifteen thousand uses of chloroform without a single death.

In the South, all medicines, including chloroform, were harder to find, so one Confederate doctor, Dr. J.J. Chisholm, invented an inhaler that used less chloroform than the cone method. The Chisholm inhaler was only about two and one-half inches long and one inch wide (see photograph). It had a plate with holes in it on the front side where the chloroform was added. At one end were two nose pieces that the surgeon could push in for storage between operations.

There was a lot of disagreement between doctors over whether anesthesia should be used. T. Longmore in his textbook on gunshot wounds thought it was very useful. He didn't agree with the Medical Inspector General who said that "the smart [pain] of the knife is a powerful stimulant." In Longmore's opinion, the pain of surgery, added to the shock of the operation and of the original injury, could kill the patient. He felt that anesthesia, by taking away part of the pain, would give the patient a better chance of survival. Confederate surgeon Edward Warren agreed with him, saying, "The discovery of the anaesthetic effects of Chloroform is the great surgical achievement of the age. Under its soothing influence operations have been performed which otherwise would have been impossible."

Samuel Gross, whose *Manual of Military Surgery* was seen as one of the most important and up-to-date books by doctors of the time, did not agree. He felt that anesthesia should be used only in very serious cases, saying: "It is astounding what little suffering the patient generally experiences, ... even from a severe wound or operation." Union surgeon Frank Hamilton, in the 1861 edition of his military surgery textbook, strongly advises doctors to use anesthesia rarely. He felt that using

This photograph shows how anesthesia was administered for surgery during the Civil War. Notice the plain wooden table for operating and the regular clothes being worn by the surgeon and steward. (Photo #CP 1563, Otis Historical Archives, National Museum of Health and Medicine, Armed Forces Institute of Pathology.)

anesthesia led to all sorts of complications after surgery. By the time the 1865 edition of his text was published, he admitted that most doctors did not agree with him about anesthesia. But he said he still believed anesthesia was the cause of so much of the gangrene and other complications seen after Civil War surgery.

The doctors who did not favor the use of anesthesia were wrong, as we now know. The 80,000 uses of chloroform during the Civil War provided the medical evidence needed to convince doctors throughout the U.S. that anesthesia should be used for all surgical procedures. The Civil War had given medicine its greatest new tool for performing surgery with far less pain and discomfort for the patient.

This Union medical kit contains several different items, including a nebulizer for local anesthesia, a syringe, and a thermometer. (Historical Collections, National Museum of Health and Medicine, Armed Forces Institute of Pathology.)

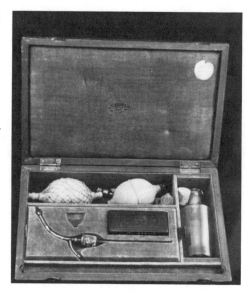

Confederate surgeon Julian Chisholm invented this inhaler to save chloroform, which was scarce in the Confederate army. The patient breathes through the nose pieces. Chloroform is poured into the plate with holes in it on top of the tiny device. (Historical Collections, National Museum of Health and Medicine, Armed Forces Institute of Pathology.)

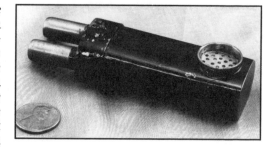

Chapter 14

MEDICINES

The Civil War was fought long before the first of the miracle drugs developed in the early 1900s. Medicines used by doctors during the Civil War did not have the scientific formula names we know today. The medicines of the Civil War era came directly from plants and herbs in nature and had names like "Fluid extract of cinchona" and "Valerian" and "Oil of turpentine." The official list of medicines to be included in the field hospital kits also included condensed milk, sugar, and black tea.

Most medicines of the time had begun as "home remedies." Medical people looking back on the medicines of the time say that only three of them were actually useful. These were quinine, used for malaria; morphine and other opiates, used for relieving pain; and chloroform, used as anesthesia in surgical operations. There were other medicines that could have been helpful but were not used in the right way or dosage. One of these is digitalis, which is used today to help the heart beat properly. It was used in the Civil War but in too small a dose. Civil War doctors used paregoric, which used alone can stop diarrhea. Since diarrhea was one of the most serious causes of death during the Civil War, this could have been a great help. Unfortunately, paregoric was always given with other drugs that actually made the diarrhea worse.

Actually, the one most commonly used drug in the Civil War was alcohol, usually in the form of whiskey. Whiskey was seen as a cure for a lot of different medical problems and it was always given to wounded soldiers at the first aid stations on the battlefield, to prevent them from going into shock. Nothing in whiskey would prevent shock but it at least was a popular drug as far as the soldiers were concerned. More whiskey was given to soldiers who would be having surgery without the anesthesia to fortify them for their operation.

Some items on the list were actually medicines that we now know are poisonous. Civil War soldiers were treated with arsenic and strychnine. One of the most commonly used medicines to stop diarrhea was a drug called calomel, which actually was a deadly mercury poison. There was a big controversy among the Civil War doctors when Surgeon General Hammond forbade the use of calomel. Hammond was eventually forced out of his job, but history did prove that his fears about calomel were justified.

Samuel Gross's *Manual of Military Surgery* listed the categories of drugs that had to be available at all military hospitals. He said that a hospital had to have anodynes (pain relievers like opium or morphine); purgatives (ipecac) to purge or clean out the system of "ill-humors" or poisons; depressants; diaphoretics to make the body sweat out poisons or "ill-humors"; diuretics to make the body rid itself of extra water; antiperiodics to stop fevers (quinine and arsenic); anesthetics for surgery (chloroform and ether); stimulants (brandy or gin); astringents to tighten tissues; and escharotics like nitric acid to burn out bad tissue and form scabs. Fortunately for the patients, many of these were never used.

The Civil War doctor usually only carried a few of his favorite medicines with him. Some, like Henry Janes

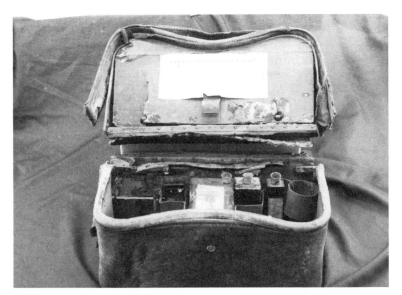

A field medicine case used in the Union army. (Historical Collections, National Museum of Health and Medicine, Armed Forces Institute of Pathology.)

This pocket medicine kit was used by Confederate surgeon J.H. Kinyon. (Historical Collections, National Museum of Health and Medicine, Armed Forces Institute of Pathology.)

from our first chapter, took an ammunition case and used it to hold small vials of the medicines he wanted to have with him all the time. Many other doctors felt the same need, and a kit holding about thirty tiny containers of medicine was made available to surgeons.

In the South, medicines were harder to obtain because at the beginning of the war, all of the pharmaceutical companies (the companies that make drugs) were in the North. The South came to rely more on gathered herbs and plants and their own remedies to make up for what they lacked. Since they generally seemed to be able to maintain adequate supplies of the three most important and effective medicines — quinine, morphine, and chloroform — by smuggling them in, it probably was better for their patients that they could not obtain most of the less effective (and sometimes dangerous) medicines.

One writer discussing Civil War medicine talked about the fact that the soldiers would take anything, as long as it tasted terrible. They assumed that if it tasted bad it had to be good for them! Reading about the medicines used, perhaps the lesson is about how critical it was to stay healthy and out of the hands of the doctors in the first place.

Chapter 15

RECOVERY

Remember the numbers — three out of every four surgical procedures were amputations. That meant that even if the wounded soldier survived the surgery and the period after surgery when so many soldiers died of infections, lockjaw, and gangrene, life was not going to return to normal quickly. For the men who had arms and legs amputated and even those who had resection surgery where their limbs were saved, their lives were still changed forever.

The recovery time was often long and hard. Soldiers recovering from wounds of their thighs would spend months in a special "bed-lift," keeping their injury completely still so it could heal. The complicated arrangement allowed the patient to be cared for while his leg and hip were immobilized.

Soldiers with arm or lower leg resections would have their injured limb immobilized in wooden splints until it healed completely. The splints had hinges on them so that they could be made to fit each patient at the exact angle the doctor wanted.

Soldiers who had their legs amputated were left with a stump. Many had artificial legs fitted, called prostheses. The number of amputations in the Civil War led to a great improvement in prosthetic devices. The artificial leg or arm had to be held in place with straps and most

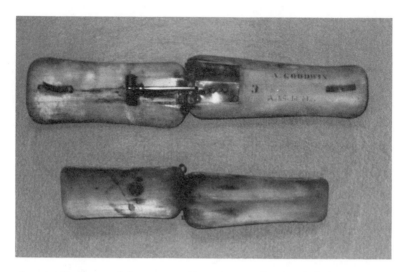

Arm splints used for supporting arms after excision surgery. Note that they can be adjusted to fit the patient. These are part of the Dr. Janes collection. (Photo by W. Michael Beller.)

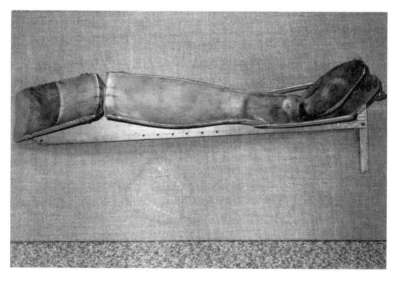

Leg splint similar to arm splint shown earlier. (Photo by W. Michael Beller.)

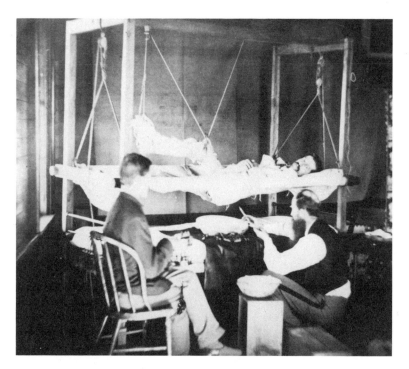

Bed-lift used for patients with injuries to their thigh bones would hold them immobile and allow the injury to heal. (Photo #CP 1623, Otis Historical Archives, National Museum of Health and Medicine, Armed Forces Institute of Pathology.)

of them were not usable in the way artificial limbs are today. The government would pay part of the cost for having the soldier's particular prosthesis made for him.

In addition to the field and general hospitals, there were also special convalescent hospitals where soldiers would go to learn how to take care of themselves in spite of their permanent disabilities. For many of the wounded soldiers of the Civil War, their pain would not end until they died many, many years later.

Captain E.B. Gates, of Pennsylvania, had to have his lower leg amputated after being wounded in July 1862. His amputation was done while he was a prisoner at Libby Prison in Richmond, Virginia. (Photo #CP 1110, Otis Historical Archives, National Museum of Health and Medicine, Armed Forces Institute of Pathology.)

Corporal David D. Cole, of New York, had his leg amputated after being shot at Amelia Court House, Virginia on April 7, 1865. He is shown fitted with an artificial leg that is tied onto the stump of his leg. (Photo #1301, Otis Historical Archives, National Museum of Health and Medicine, Armed Forces Institute of Pathology.)

Chapter 16

DEATH

When each day's battle ended, the armies would usually call a truce. Field surgeons would recover any wounded soldiers left on the field. Then would come the most unpleasant task of all. The surviving soldiers would bring back the bodies of their friends, and then they would dig their usually common graves, laying them side by side in the ground. Burials took place immediately, since there would frequently be fighting again the next day. The time for burying the dead was short. William Reed's memoir tells of looking through the ambulances and removing the dead bodies: "One by one they were placed upon stretchers, their bodies hardly cold, their limbs in every position, and they were carried out to an adjoining field where they were laid side by side."

At the time the Civil War began, the custom was to bury someone almost immediately after death. Most of the soldiers who died in the Civil War were buried where they died, far from their homes. But some families wanted their loved ones buried at home. In order to do this, there had to be some system for preserving the bodies until they could be sent home. The process of embalming dated all the way back to Egyptian times, but it had never been widely used in the U.S. before the Civil War. In the U.S., if a funeral had to be delayed, the body was packed in ice to preserve it. But that system would not work when a body had to be shipped a long way.

Embalming as a profession in the United States really came into being during the Civil War. One of the most famous embalmers was Dr. Thomas Holmes, who supposedly embalmed over four thousand soldiers during the Civil War, charging the families $100 for the service — an enormous amount of money at the time.

Embalming required its own special equipment, some of which is preserved at the National Museum of Health and Medicine. Different chemicals could be used to embalm bodies, and eleven different people applied for patents to protect their "formulas" during the 1860 to 1870 period. Some embalmers used arsenic, some used metallic salts, while others used sulfuric acid. Almost all of the embalmers worked in the Washington area and they all advertised themselves as having the best system to preserve bodies and keep them looking natural. Most of the original embalmers were doctors or pharmacists. After the embalming was completed, undertakers (people who organized funeral services) would arrange to ship the body home.

After the Civil War, the process of embalming again became less frequent. But for those families who could afford the process, embalming let them bring their soldiers home one last time. One army nurse, Mrs. Fanny Titus-Hazen of Vershire, Vermont, always made sure that families at home would know their soldiers had been cared for in their final hours. "I never failed to place by the heart of each silent soldier a bouquet of the florist's choicest flowers that the dear mother might feel assured that an earnest, sympathetic heart had ministered to her son."

Chapter 17

CHANGES IN MEDICINE DURING THE CIVIL WAR

The Civil War was a horrible time in our history. It had a great impact on the people living at that time whether they or their relatives fought in the war or not. It resulted in great change in our nation, not just the abolition of slavery, but also changes in ideas and a great movement of people around the country.

In the area of medicine during the Civil War, it is easy to sit here and look with horror at all the deaths that occurred — to know that not only did people die from the fighting but also that they died in such great numbers from disease. A visit to any Civil War battlefield park museum or to the National Museum of Medicine shows you the primitive instruments used to care for the soldiers.

But there is another way to look at medicine in the Civil War. That is to look at all the medical changes that came about because of the need to care for all those sick and wounded soldiers.

Our hospitals changed dramatically because of the Civil War. The pavilion design introduced to the U.S. during the Civil War became the model for civilian hospitals all over the country and is still used in hospital construction today.

The Civil War use of anesthesia changed surgery forever. Without the field testing done by the Civil War surgeons, both Union and Confederate, it might have taken many more years for such a marvelous development to be accepted. The addition of the Chisholm inhaler alone offered new technology for the surgical field.

The Civil War also brought about a new surgical procedure. Surgical resection or excision didn't even show up in one of the major surgical textbooks in 1861. By 1865, it rated an entire chapter. It gave surgeons an alternative way of treating persons who received shattering injuries to their arms or legs. And it led to further improvements in techniques for dealing with damaged limbs.

The Civil War opened up a whole new profession outside the home for women. Many women who had the opportunity to work in military hospitals went back and brought about changes in the civilian hospitals in their own cities and towns.

The whole process of embalming, which really developed because some families wanted to bring their soldier's body home, continued to develop (although quite slowly) after the Civil War. Eventually embalming changed the way people around the country mourned their dead.

A great deal of new medical research and technology came out of the Civil War. Many doctors carefully cataloged their cases using the new technology of photography, so that studies of procedures and care could be made.

The Civil War also helped establish the principle that medical personnel are "neutrals" and thus should never be fired upon, captured, or imprisoned. In establishing the American Red Cross after her work on the Civil War battlefields, Clara Barton would be creating the organization that came to symbolize "Stonewall" Jackson's idea of medical neutrality and aid to the entire world.

Of course, all the changes in medicine could never begin to offset the horror of the Civil War. But at least in the field of medicine, we know that something good came from the four long years of fighting and death.

Participating in Civil War medical care gave people who volunteered their efforts a chance to make at least part of the war experience a positive one. Mary Livermore, a Union nurse, said it best: "People of all conditions and circumstances, wise and unwise, rich and poor, women and men, went thither for inspiration and direction. Scenes were there enacted and deeds performed which transfigured human nature, and made it divine."

We should not forget the hardship of the soldiers suffering from wounds of battle or from disease. Looking back today, we cannot help but admire their courage in enduring what, by our modern standards, would be considered very primitive medical care. The fact that so many sick and wounded Civil War soldiers did survive is a tribute to their toughness. It is also a tribute to the efforts of the surgeons and nurses who cared for them. The efforts and sacrifices made by all the people involved should not be forgotten. Not because they did a perfectly wonderful job, but because, in the words of Confederate surgeon Deering J. Roberts, "of what was attempted and accomplished in the face of difficulties which seemed insurmountable."

SOURCES FOR RESEARCH

There is a great deal of information available on medicine during the Civil War. This book started with its photographs, and there were thousands to choose from. The collections at the National Library of Medicine and in the Otis Archives of the National Museum of Health and Medicine are incredible to work with. Choosing only a few photographs from these collections was not easy. At the National Library of Medicine, you use a card catalog and get a number to look up for the photograph you want. I never could resist looking through all the photographs around the one I wanted. In fact, I could have spent weeks just looking at their collections. The Civil War was the first war in which photography was used, and it looks like these new photographers didn't want to miss anything.

A lot of the medical tools and equipment used during the Civil War still exist. Most battlefield museums seem to have at least one medical kit on display. Many local historical societies also have medical memorabilia as part of their collections. I was lucky enough to get the chance to do more than just look at these items in a display case. At the National Museum of Health and Medicine, I was given the opportunity to hold many of the things you see pictures of in this book. It's interesting to actually hold an amputating saw, knowing what it has been used for in the past. Or to hold a piece of someone's spine with the Minié ball still stuck in it and be able to know who the person was and how he died. I was also lucky enough to find a local collection that was incredibly complete. Dr. Janes kept all his equipment and things like his uniform and boots and camp trunk. It was a real thrill to touch with my own hands these relics from the past.

The Civil War was a very important experience in the lives of the people who fought in it or who cared for the sick and wounded soldiers. So many memoirs were written by these people after the war. There was an incredible amount of material to choose from. In fact, the hardest part of writing this book was deciding what things not to use. Most of the memoirs I used were from books written in the late 1800s and they are available in university libraries. Also available in university and historical collections are many memoirs that were never published in book form at all. I have included a list of the memoirs used in this book at the end of this section. Remember that these are just a very few of the thousands of memoirs available.

Reading old medical textbooks was also quite an interesting experience. It was especially helpful to find two separate editions of the textbook by Frank Hamilton, one written in 1861 and one in 1865, so that I could compare changes in medicine over the course of the Civil War. These kinds of books are only available in historical collections at universities or medical schools because they are now so rare.

There are several sets of official reports on the Civil War, which I used quite often. The first is one that anyone writing about the Civil War always uses. This is the *War of the Rebellion: Official Records of the Union and Confederate Army*, which has over one hundred volumes and was published by the Government Printing

Office in 1889. Then there is the medical version of the Official Records, published by the Surgeon General's Office in 1875, and called the *Medical and Surgical History of the War of Rebellion*. This one is in six very large volumes. The Sanitary Commission also published its own report in 1867, entitled *Contributions Relating to the Causation and Prevention of Disease and to Camp Diseases*. Finally, there is a multi-volume set, edited by Francis Miller in 1911, called *The Photographic History of the Civil War*. This one has both photos and memoirs in it.

There were four very informative books that I read before I began this book. They helped get me started looking in the right places for information. These are: Paul Steiner's *Disease in the Civil War* (Springfield, Illinois: Charles C. Thomas, 1968); H.H. Cunningham's *Doctors in Gray* (Baton Rouge: Louisiana State University Press, 1958); George Adams's *Doctors in Blue* (New York: Henry Schuman, 1952); and Stewart Brooks's *Civil War Medicine* (Springfield, Illinois: Charles C. Thomas, 1966).

Memoirs

Boyden, Anna L. *Echoes from Hospital and White House: A Record of Mrs. Rebecca R. Pomroy's Experience in War-Times*. Boston: D. Lothrop and Company, 1884. Bucklin, Sophronia E. *In Hospital and Camp*. Philadelphia: John E. Potter and Company, 1869. Cumming, Kate. *A Journal of Hospital Life in the Confederate Army of Tennessee*. Louisville, Kentucky: John P. Morton & Co., 1866. Holland, Mary A. Gardner. *Our Army Nurses*. Boston: Lounsbery, Nichols & Worth, 1897. (This is a collection of one hundred memoirs.) Livermore, Mary A. *My Story of the War*. Hartford: A.D. Worthington and Company, 1890. Olmsted, Frederick Law. *Hospital Trans-*

ports: A Memoir. Boston: Ticknor and Fields, 1863.
Reed, William Howell. *Hospital Life in the Army of the Potomac.* Boston: William V. Spencer, 1866.

INDEX

A

Ambulances, 47-8, 49
   photo, 49
American Red Cross, 86
Amputation, 67, 69-70, 79
Anesthesia, 71-4
   photo, 73

B

Bartholow, Roberts, 23, 25
Barton, Clara, 41, 42, 86
   photo, 42
"Battle-Field Relief" wagons, 43-4
Bentley, Frederick A., photo, 30
Bickerdyke, "Mother," 41, 43
Blackwell, Elizabeth, 35
Britton, Lucius, 14-5
Bucklin, Sophronia E., 32, 45

C

Chimborazo Hospital, 51, 52, 54
   photo, 52
Chisholm, J.J., 72, 74
Chloroform inhaler, photo, 74
Cole, David D., 82
Cumming, Kate, 38, 44-5, 54, 56, 61-2, 70

D

Darcy, F., 14
Death, 17, 83-4
   embalming, 84
   numbers, 17
Disease, 17-8, 23-6
Dix, Dorothea, 35, 40-1, 42
   photo, 42

Doctors, see Surgeons
Dunster, [Dr.], 24

E

Embalming, 84
Everett, Edward, 13

F

Farnham, Amanda Colburn, 45
Field hospitals, 57-61, 62
   photos, 58, 62
Field medicine case, photo, 77
Food, 24-5
Forceps, photo, 65

G

Gates, E.B., 82
General Kearny's Brigade Hospital, photo, 34
Gross, Samuel, *Manual of Military Surgery*, 63, 72, 76

H

Hamilton, Frank, 69, 72
Hammond, [Surgeon General], 76
Hawks, Esther Hill, 35
Holmes, Thomas, 84
Hospital ships, 48-9, 50
   photo, 50
Hospital train car, model, photo, 50
Hospitals, 34, 39-40, 51-6, 57-61, 62
   convalescent camp, photo, 55
   field, 57-61, 62
      photo, 58, 62
   pavilion style, 54
   photos, 34, 52, 59
   staff, 39-40
   ventilation, 54
Howard, John A., photo, 30

I

Instruments, see Medical instruments

J

Jackson, Thomas "Stonewall," 35, 87
Janes, Henry, 13-6, 76
Jones, Daniel, 14

K

Kinyon, J.H., 77

L

Lee, Robert E., 53
Lincoln, Abraham, 13, 53
Livermore, Mary, 44, 56, 61, 87
Longmore, T., *A Treatise on Gunshot Wounds*, 19, 21, 72

M

Matrons, 39-40
McGuire, Hunter, 71-2
McLaughlin, Thomas, 15
Medical and Surgical History of the War of Rebellion, 26
Medical instruments, 63-6
  photo, 64
Medical kit, photo, 74
Medical knowledge, 19-22
  medical textbook, photos, 20
Medicines, 75-8
  home remedies, 75
Minié balls, 27, 29
  injuries from, photos, 29
Munson, Edward L., 33, 36, 66

N

National Museum of Health and Medicine, 35, 63, 84
Nurses, 39-45

O

Official Records, 15, 16
Olmsted, Frederick Law, 48-9

P

Palmer, Hannah L., 28
Piers, Stephen, 63, 64
Pocket medical kit, photos, 65, 77

R

Recovery, 79-82
  bed-lift, photo, 81
  splints, photos, 80
Reed, William Howell, 32, 48, 83
Roberts, Deering J., 37, 87
Rodenbaugh, William, photo, 31

S

Sleigh, John, photo, 68
Stewards, 38
Surgeons, 33-8
Surgery, 67-70
  exsection or resection, 69
Surgical kit, photo, 64

T

3rd Vermont Volunteers, 13
Titus-Hazen, Fanny, 84
Tompkins, Sally, 43
Transportation from battlefield to hospital, 47-50
  ambulances, 47-8
  hospital ships, 48-9
Tucker, William A., photo, 68

U

Union hospital, photo, 34
U.S. Capitol, used as hospital, photo, 52
U.S. Sanitary Commission, 23, 24, 25, 26, 37, 41, 43,
    44, 48, 53, 56, 61
  nurse, photo, 41

W

Walker, Mary Edwards, 35, 65, 66
  pocket medical kit, photo, 65
*War of the Rebellion: Official Records of the Union and
    Confederate Army*, 15, 16
Warren, Edward, 22, 72
Wounds, 27-32
Wright, Samuel C., 22